THE RIGHT CAREER PATH

Harnessing your life by choosing the right career

Anoweh bigg k

The characters and events portrayed in this book are fictitious. Any similarity to real persons, living or dead, is coincidental and not intended by the author.

ISBN-13:9798352466100

Cover design by: david

Printed in the United States of America

This book is dedicated to my young followers

CONTENTS

INTRODUCTION

Jobs and employment are among the most important current issues facing governments and societies around the world, but the question of how to align individuals and their strengths with opportunities in the world of work remains without a widely accepted, evidence-based approach.

Most career centres and government-funded employment agencies measure program results with job placement rates and program attendance figures, but these measures fail to indicate sustainable changes in individualsâ€™ careers. Tracking whether someone â€˜got the jobâ€™ says nothing about the alignment between the job and the individualâ€™s strengths, interests and life situation, nor does it say anything about that individualâ€™s ability to manage their career for the future when and if he or she leaves that first job.

Career development matters because it, and we as Career Professionals, can have a positive impact on individualsâ€™ personal attributes including hope, confidence, resilience, optimism, personal growth, and curiosity and exploration â €” when we listen to clientsâ€™ stories in new ways. Using our narrative framework, weâ€™ve found significant increases in these key personal attributes, which correlate with important career measures including career clarity, job satisfaction, job fit, and alignment between job and career expectations.

Career development â€” or perhaps a better term, â€˜Career Management Skill,â€™ â€” matters because it helps people

manage their careers for the future leading to sustainable and positive employment and career outcomes that benefit the individual and society.

I approached this by looking at career development so, before considering â€œwhy career development mattersâ€ I thought perhaps we could back up a step and focus on why â€œdevelopmentâ€ (of any sort) matters. We consider development the norm in so many life arenas other than career, using terms like â€œdevelopmentally delayedâ€ to describe an individual not progressing as expected or hoped for. â€œArrested developmentâ€ (i.e., when children stop developing as expected, after what seemed to be a normal beginning) is considered a psychological disorder. Why, then, would we expect a career to be static? People develop â€“ it makes sense that their careers would similarly develop to keep up with individualsâ€™ developmental changes.

In our Career Engagement model, we illustrate how an individual can outgrow a specific job when his or her increased capacity begins to outweigh the challenge of the position. Similarly, Csikszentmihalyi, in his work on Flow, spoke to the importance of matching skills to challenge. Career development is inherently important to achieving and maintaining Career Engagement and/or Flow. Without career development, work can become boring and meaningless. With career development, adjustments can be made to continue to achieve an optimal fit between workplace expectations and individual/organizational capacity to get the work done.

CHAPTER 1

Career

What is career?

Choosing a career can help you choose the right education and skills to support that career. Making deliberate and well-considered career decisions can increase your chances of success. It can take time and research to find the right career. In this book, we define a career, discuss various career paths, and provide advice on how to find the right career for you.

Job description

There are two definitions of career. The term "career" is frequently used to describe a profession, occupation, trade, or vocation. A career can define what you do for a living and can range from those that require extensive training and education to those that can be performed with only a high school diploma.

A high school diploma and a willingness to learn are required. Working as a doctor, lawyer, teacher, carpenter, veterinary assistant, electrician, cashier, instructor, or hairstylist could be considered a career.

However, there is another definition of a career. It also refers to your progress and actions over your working years, particularly as they pertain to your occupation. It is consists of the various occupations you've held, titles you've received, and labor you've done over a long period of time In this context, a career covers everything linked to your professional development, such as your choice of profession and promotion. Your single career could take you down a number of different paths.

Different types of professional trajectories

There are various types of professional route available.

Multiple unrelated jobs: Your career may consist of several occupations that are unrelated to one another. You could, for example, work as a sales associate in a retail setting, then as a waiter in a restaurant, and finally as a receptionist at a veterinary clinic. Because each job is so unique, it is impossible to forecast what your next employment will be. Because they have relatively little in common, you may not notice big income rises or increases in responsibility from one to the next.

Advancing within one occupation: This approach entails advancing inside the same occupation, whether you work for the same organization or for different ones. For instance, if you work as a cashier, you are advancing in the same industry but not in the same occupation: This approach entails remaining in the same industry but not necessarily in the same occupation. For example, if you want to be a restaurant manager, you could start as a dish washer, then advance to a server position, then head server or assistant management, and finally manager.

Career Path Examples

Reviewing career paths for a range of various jobs might help you understand how career paths can grow. Be aware that some career pathways, such as those that advance inside one occupation, are direct, but others are indirect and may include working in multiple industries or jobs.

Sales and customer service: Customer service representative

> inner sales rep > outdoor salesperson > account executive > sales manager

Editorial positions include editorial assistant, assistant editor, editor, senior editor, and editorial director.

Curriculum coordinator -> teacher -> assistant principal -> principal

Sales associate -> assistant manager -> shop manager -> regional manager in retail

Human resources: HR assistant -> HR specialist -> assistant director of human resources -> director of human resources

The Distinction Between A Job And A Career

While both jobs and careers allow us to earn enough money to live on,they do not mean the same thing: support ourselves and our families. To plan your professional goals, you must first choose if you are seeking for a job or a career.

What exactly is a job?

A job is something that you do to earn money to meet your fundamental necessities. It might be a full-time or part-time job, and it can be temporary. Instead of a salary with benefits, you could receive an hourly wage or a fixed income. You may need to study certain skills related to that profession, but not all careers necessitate a specialist degree or advanced training.

Companies expect their employees to do their respective jobs in exchange for regular remuneration and to be accountable for the responsibilities assigned to them

.A job can also be defined as a short- or long-term agreement between an employer and a worker. For example, a business may employ a local contractor to finish an office refurbishment project. They reach an agreement on payment conditions, and the task is completed once the project is completed.

What exactly is a career?

A career is a long-term professional journey that you might choose based on your interests. It is the road you take in order to achieve your professional goals and desires. These objectives may necessitate a certain amount of education or training. Individuals pursuing careers frequently have fixed salaries that include benefits such as stock options, retirement plans, pensions, and bonuses. They also obtain non-monetary rewards such as personal pride, job fulfillment, and self-worth.

A career might last your entire life. You could work for a variety of employers in your chosen industry as you advance in your career.

What impact does your job have on your career?

Even if you don't have a certain professional path in mind when you first enter the workforce, you will most likely hold a variety of jobs during your lifetime. It may be beneficial to think of each position you hold as a step in your life's work. Your employment can have the following effects on your career:

Your career is made up of jobs.

A career is made up of all of the jobs you've had, regardless of whether they're related. You could spend decades working in the same department for the same company.

Alternatively, you could work a variety of seemingly unconnected occupations during your career, such as greenskeeper, executive assistant, and information technology specialist. They all help to define your career and connect you with other options that interest you. Consider work to be short-term responsibilities that can assist you attain your long-term objectives.

Each job teaches you something new.

Every work teaches you lessons that you can use to future ones. You will also acquire a wide range of skills, knowledge, and experiences. For example, perhaps your previous career as a retail clerk taught you how to handle unpleasant situations with grace. You may have learned good communication and customer service skills while working as a receptionist. Other roles could help you improve your writing skills or your ability to manage people.can teach you the importance of perseverance and hard work

Jobs give opportunities for networking.

With each employment, you establish a professional network and community. Maintaining a constructive and professional relationship with all of your coworkers and clients will allow you to reach out to these relationships throughout your career.

Working hard pays off.

Your current employment may have an unanticipated impact on your career. As a result, attempt to go above and above the minimal minimum. A cheerful attitude, enthusiasm to learn, and consistently high-quality work can set you apart, open doors to new chances, and get you recommendations for future positions.

4 Ways to Make a Job a Career

If you want to pursue a career,

You can work toward your long-term goal. These tactics can be beneficial.

1. Continue To Learn And Grow

Always strive to improve your abilities and knowledge. Determine what expertise and experience you will require to advance in your chosen job path. Once you've identified the needs, look for ways to improve your skills, whether through on-the-job training or formal training, online courses, and education. Look to successful individuals in that field to identify which talents will benefit your career the most. Consider their abilities, talents, and accomplishments. Reach out to others in comparable fields and get their advice.

2. Find A Mentor.

Seek out a mentor or two who have a higher-level position or experience in your desired field. Inquire if they will consider professionally assisting and counseling you. You can prepare specific questions to ask or topics to discuss with a mentor while working with them. Consider your mentor's route and whether a similar one could be appropriate for you.

.

3.Broaden Your Network

Workshops, conferences, seminars, and social gatherings are excellent places to network with people in your area. You can broaden your network in order to have additional resources for sharing your experiences.long-term ambitions The abilities and knowledge you gain in each function can help you advance in your career.

CHAPTER 2

Types of career

Careers are diverse; they are divided into 13 categories. Choosing a career path is easier when you understand your options. Knowing about the numerous professional categories can enable you to select the best employment for your talents, education, and interests. This page will provide a list of typical professional fields as well as examples of employment within each category.

Architecture and engineering

Architects are professionals who plan and design buildings and parks. However, architecture encompasses a considerably broader range of disciplines, from software to restoration, landscapes to freeways. If you want to work as an accountant,

Your career as an architect might take many different paths. In this essay, we will look at 19 different types of architects as well as other relevant occupations to consider.

What exactly is an architect?

Architecture is the art and discipline of designing a structure, space, or other environment for people to utilize for a certain purpose. An architect is a professional who plans, designs, and supervises project construction. There are numerous job paths available in architecture. Some have a larger scope, while others require a more specific skill set. Whatever field you pick, you will eventually use a variety of technical, technological, and design ideas to fulfill your job.

Why Study Architecture?

Architects are creative problem solvers that like building structures and ideas that boost efficiency and optimize environments for communities, homeowners, and enterprises. These specialists envisage projects based on client specifications and generate designs and blueprints to bring those visions to life.

Time management, communication, and quantitative skills are required for architects. They must also be capable of working well in leadership roles and be adaptable to changing styles and regulations.

Architecture Career Opportunities

1. Landscape Architect

Designing outdoor landscapes, encompassing infrastructure, public areas, agriculture, and forestry, is critical not just for establishing the webs that connect our urban and rural settings, but also, and perhaps more crucially, for responding to globalization and climate change

2. Urban Designer

The conditions of urbanism are continually changing as a result of a rapidly expanding percentage of our population relocating into cities. The urban environment's changing status makes it an intriguing path to explore as an architect, spanning everything from economic and demographic changes to sustainable development. It is a necessary but difficult task within our profession; it necessitates adaptability and large-scale problem solutions.

3. Architect For Restoration

The heritage and history of our civilizations as represented by architecture are not only magnificent vistas into the past, but also critical to comprehending our culture as a profession. Building conservation and restoration are clearly difficult tasks; it is impossible to please everyone. The news media despite the often highly attractive solutions, the procedure of restoration is frequently referred as as a "heritage murder."

4. Architect Of Research

Our techniques of representation and expression are changing tremendously as a result of the current wave of digital design and the ongoing progress of digital tools. The impact of information technology on architecture has been tremendous, and it is far from over. These continuous advances are made possible in part by the interesting research being conducted by architects, which does not necessarily consist of constructing buildings, but rather focuses on how these new tools may better our job.

5. Architect Of Lighting

Light has a huge effect on our emotional and physical wellbeing, as anyone who lives at high latitudes understands. Investigating lighting design encompasses increasing the quality of our experiences, our health and well-being, and the sustainability of not just the natural environment, but also smaller scale environments.areas, such as our workplaces

6. Political Architect

Some argue that architecture is by nature political, however being active in the political decision of a city or country is a different story. Architecture is more than just creating beautiful objects; the discipline has a value in organizing society. Architecture firm Terroir, for example, has worked with the Burnie City Council as well as with the Parramatta City Council in Australia, to argue for a specific structure for the city, to foresee what would happen, and to develop a set of criteria for the city's evolution It is an example of architecture influencing politics rather than politics affecting architecture.

7. Extreme Designer

Extreme weather events such as floods, heat waves, and storms are expected to become more often as climate change progresses. Existing severe settings, such as deserts, are likely to grow as a result of phenomena like desertification. Being an architect who specializes in extreme weather conditions is thus not only an extraordinarily fascinating way to approach the subject, but also crucial in helping us adapt to our planet's future.

Art and design careers

If, after graduation, you realize that architecture is not for you,Design and art, on the other hand, might be. Architecture is already a type of design (or is it the other way around?), making it easy to draw parallels between your education as an architect and your career as an artist or designer. Combining two fields, such as graphic design and architecture, is another option. Perhaps your passion is making it easier for architects to communicate visually?

8. Artist

Despite the fact that Olafur Eliasson did not study architecture, he collaborates with numerous architects at Studio Olafur Eliasson, demonstrating how harmonious and necessary the interaction between space and art is. The spatial thinking and visualization skills acquired during an architecture education are ideal for installation art, sculpture, and spatial experiences that do not require functioning.

9. Designer Of Industrial Products

Due to their intimate creative relationships, several architecture firms have moved out into industrial design. However, as opposed to large-scale buildings developed for a specific setting, industrial design concentrates on lower scale objects of mass manufacture. If the notion of creating something massive, permanent, and landscape changing sounds too daunting, industrial design is a terrific, lesser scaled option.

10. Designer Of Furniture

Furniture design, more than industrial design, can be considered architecture's little sister. Countless famous architects, including Charles and Ray Eames, Alvar Aalto, and Arne Jacobsen, have made significant contributions to furniture design. Contemporary architects, such as Zaha Hadid Architects, are following suit, demonstrating that the two can be done concurrently.

11. Designer Of Textiles

Textile design necessitates sensitivity to color, tactility, construction, patterns, and forms, all of which are developed during any architecture student's years in school. As the two merge, the relationship between "skin" and structure is more literal than that of a building. In many ways, high fashion is reminiscent of architecture, adopting the geometric and sculptural constructions of modern buildings.

12. Designer Of Graphics

Graphic design is how we perceive and identify our surroundings. It is extremely useful for communication. It can also be so visually appealing that one cannot help but want to become a graphic designer. Taking a short course in graphic design to supplement a degree in architecture can open up a variety of opportunities to continue working in the field while taking charge of tasks that are more suited to your communication interests.

13. Designer Of Video Games

Designing a virtual world with near-limitless boundaries may be one of the most enjoyable things a newly graduated architect could do with their education. Constructing the architecture of a video game allows you to let your imagination run wild while also adding depth to your spatial reasoning allowing your imagination to run wild, but it may also add depth to your spatial reasoning.

14. Photographer

Architecture photography is growing in popularity, possibly due to the beautiful geometry that can emerge when something is constrained within a lens. Photography is more concerned with the aesthetic, with the object and the composition in that one-of-a-kind moment, within that one-of-a-kind frame. It is more concerned with the passing atmosphere than with the permanent organization of people and spaces. Nonetheless, it is made up of composition, color, environment, and experiences.

15. Designer Of Production

Although a set or a stage are much smaller platforms than a virtual planet, designing theater and film sets allows for the same level of creativity. It relieves the pressures of traditional spatial design and expression, allowing for more evocative, sensual, and story-driven experiences while still utilizing all of the knowledge and skills gained from an architecture education: time constraints, conceptual environments, and collaborative creativity.

Careers Other Than Design

If you find yourself shaking your head at any mention of architecture, art, or design while scrolling through this list, this final list is for you. It covers six careers outside of the stereotypical design fields, mostly in the human sciences, because architecture is inherently focused on the human experience. Taking the essence of your architectural education and applying it to another discipline may even make you a stronger professional candidate, the human condition Taking the essence of your architectural education and applying it to another discipline may even make you a stronger professional candidate.

16. Teacher/Professor

Young teachers at architecture schools are becoming more common, and if you want to learn more about the field before deciding whether or not to stay in it, a year or two of teaching could be an excellent way to do so. Teaching is a two-way street, especially at such a young age, and it provides you with an excellent opportunity to learn from your students while also reflecting on your own perspective on architecture. Here are some pointers to help you succeed as a young professor.

17. Philanthropist

Historically, architecture was a gentleman's profession, pursued as a philanthropic endeavor rather than a commercial one. Women have begun to gain a strong hold on the profession today, but the philanthropic ideal has thankfully not died out. Contemporary architecture must prioritize sustainability on multiple levels: environmental, social, psychological, and economic. If you are interested in other types of philanthropy, you can use your knowledge and awareness of these ideals. It is never a waste of time to establish a sustainable foundation with a humanitarian goal.to gain a firm grip on the profession.to gain a firm grip on the profession, but thankfully, the philanthropic ideal has not perished. Contemporary architecture must prioritize sustainability on multiple levels: environmental, social, psychological, and economic. If you are interested in other types of philanthropy, you can use your knowledge and awareness of these ideals.

18. Politician

As previously stated, architecture and politics are inextricably linked in many ways. The knowledge one gains about people and how they interact with their environment, how they are organized, and what makes the human body and psyche feel at ease; all of these skills contribute significantly to making a good politician. In fact, Anders Adlercreutz, a current first-term Member of Parliament in Finland, was educated as an architect and practiced for many years before entering politics, whereas Richard Rogers serves in the House of Lords while running his practice.

19. Conservationist

Conservation of the environment, like philanthropy, is becoming a focal point within architecture. Despite numerous efforts, our planet is still on a path that will lead to disaster in terms of our natural surroundings. Using your knowledge of spatial organization to develop an environmental conservation method is not only intellectually stimulating, but also vital to our society.

20. Writer

Using an architectural education to become a writer or journalist can be a great way to put it to use; we learn to articulate ourselves using (mostly) descriptive language and rhetoric in order to communicate our complex projects to teachers and critics. Making that into writing, whether fictional or nonfiction, is another way of creating a different world and experience for others. Despite the fact that the print is two-dimensional, the stories are not.

21. Entrepreneur

Problem solving, creative thinking, and the art of persuasion are three skills that architects and entrepreneurs share and that you can leverage. Your experience with abstract concepts and human interaction can make you a stronger competitor with an alternative way of thinking.

CHAPTER 3

Culture, arts, and entertainment

This profession is dedicated to improving people's lives through culture, the sharing of arts, and self-expression. These professions have formal educational programs, but they also include self-taught individuals with natural talent.

If you consider yourself to be creative, you may be wondering how you can apply your skills to a job that will both excite you and provide you with enough money to live comfortably. While artistic jobs can be competitive to obtain and financially difficult to maintain, many careers offer both stability and the opportunity to use your creative talents on a daily basis. In this article, we will discuss jobs in the creative arts that will allow you to turn your passion into a rewarding career.

What exactly are creatives?

Individuals who use their talents to create something unique through creative expression are referred to as creatives. Visual and theatrical arts, written and musical expression, and other creative pursuits are all practiced by creative people. They have an innate desire to create something new in order to share ideas, inspire others, and entertain an audience. Work is often viewed as another outlet for creatives, and they are often most fulfilled when they can devote their lives to their art.

1:Artist Professional

To begin with, and perhaps most obviously, there is no reason why you cannot pursue a career as a professional artist if you have talent and dedication. As this is a highly competitive career path, you will also need a lot of self-confidence, stamina, and the ability to promote yourself.

Relevant work experience in the creative sector, such as working as a studio assistant, would be advantageous, and you should be resourceful in finding new and interesting places to showcase and sell your work in order to establish your reputation. Some artists choose to continue developing their work while working in a related full- or part-time job, such as that of an art teacher/tutor.

Many careers offer both stability and the opportunity to use your creative talents on a daily basis, despite being competitive to earn and financially challenging to keep. In this article, we will discuss jobs in the creative arts that will allow you to turn your passion into a rewarding career.

If you have talent and dedication, you can pursue a career as a professional artist, which is perhaps the most obvious of art careers. As this is a highly competitive career path, you will also need a lot of self-confidence, stamina, and the ability to promote yourself.

Relevant work experience in the creative sector, such as working as a studio assistant, would be advantageous, and you should be resourceful in finding new and interesting places to showcase and sell your work in order to establish your reputation. Some artists choose to continue developing their work while working in a related full- or part-time job, such as that of an art teacher/tutor

2:Illustrator

Illustrators use their artistic abilities to communicate stories, messages, or ideas to a specific audience. They typically work freelance for a variety of clients and are likely to specialize in a particular medium, such as drawing, photography, or digital illustration. In this case, your portfolio should show that you can work to a specific brief, such as designing a book cover.

You should also demonstrate your ability to work in a variety of formats, especially computer-aided design (CAD) techniques. A postgraduate degree in fine arts with a concentration in illustration should provide you with a wide range of relevant skills to offer prospective employers.

3:Photographer

Photographers use a variety of tools to capture images in the style and brief specified by a client or the employer .Photography can be used for a variety of purposes and specializations, ranging from weddings to advertising, photojournalism, and more. Some fields, such as fashion photography, are extremely competitive, and you may face difficulties.

It is advantageous to have a Master of Fine Arts in photography.

Along with working on your portfolio, you should look for opportunities to network, have your work published, and gain new skills and experience by volunteering, work shadowing, or participating in work experience and project work with photographers or relevant employers.

4:Animator

An animator creates a series of images known as frames, which when combined create the illusion of movement known as animation. Animators may work on a film's visual effects team or in advertising, among other things. This is another competitive area, and your portfolio would be in the form of a brief but effective showreel - either a DVD or an online portfolio video to improve A postgraduate specialization in animation would improve your employability, but it is not required. To become an animator, you must have artistic talent as well as strong technical skills and an eye for detail.

5:Designer Of Graphics

A graphic designer is in charge of developing design solutions with a strong visual impact. Working to a brief agreed upon with the client, creative director, or account manager is part of the job.

Graphic designers create creative ideas and concepts, selecting the appropriate media and style to achieve the client's goals. It is very beneficial to become a graphic designer if you have specialized in design (or an aspect of design) in your degree and mastered the skills required, such as the use of computer packages such as Photoshop. You might also think about continuing your education at the postgraduate level with a Master of Design (MDes).

6:Curator

As a curator, you will be in charge of exhibit collections in a gallery or museum, deciding how to best present an exhibition to the public, raising funds and grants, collaborating with institutions or artists, and ensuring that collections are properly preserved. Curators work in a wide variety of fields,a variety of mediums, ranging from contemporary audio-visual artworks to ancient sculpture The field is often very competitive, so you might consider a postgraduate qualification in a subject such as museum studies.

7:Printmaker

Printmakers make art with printing presses, usually on paper, and they usually work to specific briefs. Etching, block printing, woodcuts, silkscreening, and lithography are some of the techniques used, with electronic and digital processes becoming more popular. Following a degree in fine arts, you may discover that printmaking is your preferred medium, especially if you specialize in design or illustration. To improve your employability (especially if you are unemployed),If you decide to go self-employed, look for relevant work experience opportunities and build a network of relevant contacts in person and online.

8:Art Instructor/University Lecturer

A career as an art teacher could be extremely rewarding if you want to use your passion for art to motivate and inspire young people while also encouraging the development of budding talents. To teach at the primary/secondary level in most countries, you will need a teaching qualification, and to teach at the university level, you will need a postgraduate degree.

To effectively teach and inspire your students, you should also have a lot of confidence and excellent communication and presentation skills. You could also teach private art lessons to individuals or small groups, or you could specialize in one area.as in art therapy

9:Actors

Actors use theater, film, television, and other forms of performing arts to express themselves and play characters. They analyze a script written by a writer to entertain or inform an audience

Actors work in a variety of settings, such as production studios, theaters, and theme parks, as well as on location. Work assignments are typically brief, ranging from a few days to a few months.

10:Choreographers And Dancers

Dance performances are used by dancers and choreographers to express ideas and stories. Ballet, tango, modern dance, tap, and jazz are just a few examples of dance styles.

Some dancers work for performing arts companies or on their own. Choreographers can work in dance schools or as independent contractors.

11.Composers And Music Directors

Music directors, also known as conductors, are in charge of orchestras and other musical ensembles during performances and recording sessions. Composers create original music in a wide range of musical styles.

The majority of music directors work for religious organizations and schools, or they work for themselves Music directors may spend a significant amount of time traveling to various performances. Composers can work from home, offices, or recording studios.

12.Singers And Musicians

Musicians and singers perform live and in recording studios by playing instruments or singing. They perform in a wide range of styles, such as classical, jazz, opera, hip-hop, and rock music

Musicians and singers frequently perform in concert halls, arenas, and clubs.

13.Directors And Producers

Producers and directors create films, television shows, live theater, commercials, and other forms of performing arts. They adapt a writer's script in order to entertain or inform an audience.

Producers and directors are constantly under pressure to complete their projects on time. Producers and directors' work hours can be long and irregular.

CHAPTER 4

Agriculture, food, and natural resource careers

Companies that specialize in farming, food production, and natural resource management and protection offer the following careers.

1.Agricola Engineer

Apply engineering technology and biological science knowledge to agricultural problems with regard to power and machinery, electrification, structures, soil and water conservation, and so on and agricultural product processing

2.Operators Of Agricultural Equipments

and control agricultural equipment to aid in activities such as tilling soil, planting, cultivating, and harvesting crops, feeding and herding livestock, and removing animal waste. Crop baling and hay bucking are examples of tasks that may be performed. Post-harvest tasks such as husking, shelling, threshing, and ginning may be performed using stationary equipment.

3.Agricultural Employees

All agricultural workers who are not individually listed.

4: Breeders Of Animals

Choose and breed animals based on their ancestry, characteristics, and offspring. Knowledge of artificial insemination techniques and equipment use may be required. Keeping records on heats, birth intervals, or pedigree may be required.

5: Animal Watchers

Feed, water, groom, bathe, exercise, or otherwise care for pets and other non-raised animals to promote and maintain their well-being.Dogs, cats, race horses, ornamental fish or birds, zoo animals, and mice are examples of animals raised for human consumption. Work in kennels, animal shelters, zoos, circuses, and aquariums, among other places. Records of feedings, treatments, and animals received or discharged may be kept. Cages, pens, and fish tanks may be cleaned, disinfected, and repaired.

6.Scientist In Animal Research

Conduct genetics, nutrition, reproduction, growth, and development research on domestic farm animals.

7.Technicians In Biology

Assist biological and medical researchers. Setting up, operating, and maintaining laboratory instruments and equipment, monitoring experiments, collecting data and samples, making observations, and calculating and recording results Organic substances such as blood, food, and drugs may be analyzed.

8.Clinical Research Coordinators

Clinical research projects are planned, directed, or coordinated. Direct the activities of clinical research project workers engaged in clinical research projects to ensure compliance with protocols and overall clinical objectives. May evaluate and analyze clinical data .

CHAPTER 5

FARMWORKERS AND LABORERS, CROP, NURSERY, AND GREENHOUSE

Manually plant, cultivate, and harvest vegetables, fruits, nuts, horticultural specialties, and field crops. Use hand tools, such as shovels, trowels, hoes, tampers, pruning hooks, shears, and knives. Duties may include tilling soil and applying fertilizers; transplanting, weeding, thinning, or pruning crops; applying pesticides; or cleaning, grading, sorting, packing, and loading harvested products. May construct trellises, repair fences and farm buildings, or participate in irrigation activities.

Food Scientists And Technologists

Use chemistry, microbiology, engineering, and other sciences to study the principles underlying the processing and deterioration of foods; analyze food content to determine levels of vitamins, fat, sugar, and protein; discover new food sources; research ways to make processed foods safe, palatable, and healthful; and apply food science knowledge to determine best ways to process, package, preserve, store, and distribute food

Forest And Conservation Technicians

Provide technical assistance regarding the conservation of soil, water, forests, or related natural resources. May compile data pertaining to size, content, condition, and other characteristics of forest tracts under the direction of foresters, or train and lead forest workers in forest propagation and fire prevention and suppression. May assist conservation scientists in managing, improving, and protecting rangelands and wildlife habitats

Foresters

Manage public and private forested lands for economic, recreational, and conservation purposes. May inventory the type, amount, and location of standing timber, appraise the timber's worth, negotiate the purchase, and draw up contracts for procurement. May determine how to conserve wildlife habitats, creek beds, water quality, and soil stability, and how best to comply with environmental regulations. May devise plans for planting and growing new trees, monitor trees for healthy growth, and determine optimal harvesting schedules.

Natural Sciences Managers

Plan, direct, or coordinate activities in such fields as life sciences, physical sciences, mathematics, statistics, and research and development in these fields.

CHAPTER 6

Careers in BUSINESS MANAGEMENT AND ADMINISTRATION.

1 Client Services Managers

Client services managers are responsible for developing and implementing customer service procedures and training staff to follow the established guidelines. They keep in contact with current clients and talk to them about campaigns or projects they might be interested in. Client services managers help customers with questions and inquiries and resolve issues as needed.

2 Sales Representative

Sales representatives contact new or existing customers and discuss products or services they may be interested in. They negotiate contracts and follow up with clients to ensure their satisfaction with the service. Sales representatives could also prospect potential clients. They sometimes act as customer service representatives and help clients with questions or issues with products. Sales representatives may work with individuals, businesses or other organizations.

3 Project Manager

Primary duties: Project managers (PMs) organize, plan, direct and coordinate business projects and are responsible that all projects are completed according to deadline, budget and company goals. They are in charge of supervising teams, scheduling meetings, troubleshooting and measuring small goals and milestones according to the larger goal.

4 Office Manager

An office manager organizes business operations, procedures and overall maintenance. They prepare payroll and approve supply requests. An office manager might have an administrative team to which they assign duties and manage tasks. Office managers should be familiar with an office environment and how to manage other people.

5. Human Resource Manager

Human resource managers are responsible for overseeing all aspects of employee hiring, firing, payroll, training and development and governance. They are often in charge of researching and recruiting employees, coordinating interviews and onboarding new hires. Human resource managers handle payroll, benefits and may be in charge of incentive programs if the company offers them.

7 Business Manager

A business manager is responsible for supervising and managing the business of a company, including assets, operations and employees. Tasks will vary by company size but the main goals of the business manager is to evaluate, troubleshoot and implement business strategies for optimum company productivity and efficiency.

8 Staff Accountant

A staff accountant is responsible for maintaining financial reports, records, general ledgers, preparation and analysis of budgets and general bookkeeping. They may also prepare invoices and account reconciliation. Staff accountants develop and implement accounting procedures for the organization.

9. Marketing Manager

A marketing manager works with executives to develop a strategy for their company to drive more sales and sign customers. They often analyze data for industry trends in regards to the products or services their company supplies. A marketing manager may supervise a team of marketing coordinators and help to train and develop their team for future growth.

10. Business Consultant

Primary duties: A business consultant organizes and executes different administrative assignments for a client. They gather client and business information through research, interviews and other methods to find the strengths and weaknesses of the organization. Business consultants, then, discuss these findings with their clients and provide ideas and solutions to issues found during the assessment.

11. Development Director

Primary duties: A development director works with an organization to create a strategic plan to raise funds for the company. The plan needs to be cost-effective and is usually time-sensitive. Their primary focus is to oversee fundraising efforts, including delegating tasks and duties to team members. Development directors often network and make connections with potential donors or sponsors

CHAPTER 7

Careers in education and training

Teaching

Teaching is certainly the most commonly known career path for students earning a degree in education, and it's a great option if you like working with children or adults in a classroom setting. Teachers prepare and educate their students for the world. Their subject matter depends on the age they are instructing, ranging from math and reading basics up until specialty courses taught in higher education. Teachers also have the ability to work in different environments; primarily traditional schools but also online options.

Education Administration

Some teachers who are looking for an opportunity for growth within their school community can pursue an advanced degree to become an educational administrator. A Master's Degree in Education Administration, for example, can prepare you to help fellow teachers align their lesson plans with district, state and federal materials and requirements, as well as design standalone programs, such as a school safety program.

School Counseling

School counselors help students socially, academically and

emotionally, as well as guide them along their path to college or into the workforce.

School Social Work

A school social worker is an important part of the education system in that they help behavior issues within students and ultimately aid in their educational success. And, according to government data, there is a growing need for social workers.

CHAPTER 8

Careers in government and public administration

Foreign Service

Foreign Service workers serve as representatives of a country in its embassies, consulates, and diplomatic missions around the world. People in Foreign Service positions are not elected, rather, they apply for or are appointed to their posts. Work in Foreign Service is divided into four areas: administration (workers who manage country's agencies abroad); consular affairs (workers who provide medical, legal, and other services to the country's . citizens traveling abroad); economic and commercial affairs (workers who study foreign economies and how they might affect the country); and political affairs (workers who study the impact of U.S. and foreign political changes). Workers in this area, as in many areas of government, are subject to extensive background screening. Jobs in Foreign Service include ambassadors, cultural officers, and Foreign Service officers.

Governance C

This pathway includes all of the officials who are elected and appointed to national, state, and local offices. Workers in this area, including the president, members of Congress, and mayors, create and implement public policy and laws. This pathway also includes the many support and administrative workers who help officials perform their jobs. Jobs in this area include appointed and elected officials, city managers, congressional aides, and lobbyists.

National Security

The careers in this pathway are all based in the armed services. Our system of national security is a complex one that demands people with all types of skills, such as business, medical, legal, mechanical, and many more. A career in the army, navy, air force, Marine Corps, Coast Guard, or National Guard involves rigorous training and a hefty commitment of time and energy. But job satisfaction is often quite high in this field, which presents opportunities for almost every interest. Jobs in this area include cryptographic technicians, intelligence officers, mechanical engineers, and military pilots.

Planning Pathways

People who work in the planning pathway make decisions about how to best use land and resources. They take a look at many factors, including population, industry, and traffic patterns, and figure out how to use an area's resources for the greatest benefit and with the least harm to the environment. They give their plans and recommendations to officials or legislative bodies, who then decide whether or not to implement or refine them. Jobs in this pathway include business managers, city planners, and statisticians.

Public Management And Administration

Careers in this pathway deal with the budgeting, management, and staffing of agencies and offices that deal with public resources. There are strict and complex rules that govern this field. Workers here must have a firm grasp on these rules and their own obligations to the public in their work. Jobs in this pathway include city managers, court clerks, and purchasing managers.

Regulation Pathway

Work in the regulation pathway requires knowledge of a certain industry or area, such as construction, coupled with a knowledge of the laws and regulation that apply to that industry. Workers in this area make sure that buildings are up to fire codes, that manufacturers are not harming the environment when they dispose of wastes, and that airlines are adhering to the latest safety and security measures. Examples of careers in regulation include aviation safety inspectors, bank examiners, and fire safety inspectors.

Revenue And Taxation

Revenue and taxation professionals work with taxes and tax laws. They collect and monitor taxes, perform audits, review tax returns, and keep track of fines for overdue taxes. People who work in this pathway must stay up-to-date on tax laws, which change from year to year. Revenue and tax professionals must be good with money and numbers and are responsible for a great deal of private and sensitive information. Examples of careers in the revenue and taxation pathway are auditors, tax attorneys, and employees of the Internal Revenue Service.

CHAPTER 9

Careers in health science and medicine

Biomedical Scientist

Biomedical scientists work with patients and in labs to find new ways to cure or treat disease with diagnostic tools or therapeutic strategies. They work at diagnosing diseases and illnesses such as HIV, cancer, diabetes, food poisoning, hepatitis and meningitis.

Histology Technician

A histology technician works in a medical lab and focuses on coverting tissue samples into microscope slides for disease diagnosis. This role is vital in the diagnosis and treatments of diseases like cancer. They work behind the scenes to supply doctors with important information.

Histology technicians work with pathologists and lab managers on a daily basis.

Pathologist

Pathology is the study of disease - what causes the disease and its effect on the human body. Pathologists work in labs to study bodily fluids and tissue samples. They provide vital information to help doctors diagnose disease. Some pathologists also perform autopsies to determine cause of death and disease progression.

Pharmacist

They ensure that the supply of medicines is within the law. ensuring that the medicines prescribed to patients are suitable. advising patients about medicines, including how to take them, what reactions may occur and answering patients' questions.

Neurologist

A Neurologist's responsibilities include diagnosing and treating disorders of the brain, spinal cord and nervous system. This requires a Neurologist to order tests and evaluate results to provide proper care to their patients.

Medical Doctors

Medical doctors Extend primary care and chronic care clinics. Offer emergency or triage care. Classify and reply to emergency situations and offer professional and care.

CHAPTER 10

Careers in information technology

1. It Technician

An IT technician collaborates with support specialists to analyze and diagnose computer issues. They also monitor processing functions, install relevant software and perform tests on computer equipment and applications when necessary. They may also train a company's employees, clients and other users on a new program or function as well.

IT technicians must earn an associate degree in IT or a bachelor's degree in computer science or networking. Technicians render services for IT companies depending on the industry they choose to work in and may need to learn more about database programming to give themselves an advantage in an entry-level role.

2. Support Specialist

Support specialists are responsible for reviewing and solving computer network and hardware problems for a business. They can work in a variety of industries to provide general support to a company's employees or at a technology or software-as-a-service (SaaS) company to provide technical support on user experience issues that require technical assistance.

Support specialists typically obtain a bachelor's degree in IT or computer science. Having a certificate or an associate degree paired with relevant professional experience may also be acceptable.

3. Quality Assurance Tester

Quality assurance testers are technicians or engineers who check software products to see if they're up to industry standards and free of any issues. This role is common for gaming systems, mobile applications and other technology that needs further testing and maintenance when recommended.

Many quality assurance testers have a bachelor's degree in software design, engineering or computer science. Testers can work on different software for IT companies, which may influence what degree or specialization they pursue. These professionals should also have excellent time management and communication skills to help document test cases.

4. Web Developer

Web developers design the appearance, navigation and content organization of a website. They use coding languages such as HTML, CSS and JavaScript to manage graphics, applications and content that address a client's needs.

Many web developers earn an associate degree in web development or other relevant IT field. Some may pursue a bachelor's degree in IT or another business field. Others may develop their web design skills through certificate programs or self-paced learning. To secure employment, previous experience and a portfolio of work are often required.

5. It Security Specialist

: IT security specialists work in various industries to build and maintain digital protective measures on intellectual property and data that belong to an organization. They help companies create contingency plans in case information gets hacked from their networks and servers. These professionals also create strategies to troubleshoot problems as they arise.

A bachelor's degree or professional certification is often required. Courses may involve math, programming and operating systems and certifications offered by the Information Systems Security Certification Consortium (ISC2).

6. Computer Programmer

Primary duties: A computer programmer is someone who writes new computer software using coding languages like HTML, JavaScript and CSS. Video game software can be updated to improve online gameplay, which is an opportunity for programmers to troubleshoot problems experienced by gamers after the game is released to the general public.

7.Software Engineer

Software engineers apply their knowledge of mathematics and computer science to create and improve new software. They may work on enterprise applications, operating systems and network control systems, which are all examples of software that can be used to help businesses scale their IT infrastructure.

CHAPTER 11

Careers in law , public safety, correction and security

Administrative Law Judges, Adjudicators, And Hearing Officers

Conduct hearings to recommend or make decisions on claims concerning government programs or other government-related matters. Determine liability, sanctions, or penalties, or recommend the acceptance or rejection of..

Arbitrators, Mediators, and Conciliators

Facilitate negotiation and conflict resolution through dialogue. Resolve conflicts outside of the court system by mutual consent of parties involved

Criminal Investigators And Special Agents

Investigate alleged or suspected criminal violations of Federal, state, or local laws to determine if evidence is sufficient to recommend prosecution

Criminal Justice And Law Enforcement Teachers, Postsecondary

Teach courses in criminal justice, corrections, and law enforcement administration. Includes both teachers primarily engaged in teaching and those who do a combination of teaching and research.

Crossing Guards And Flaggers

Guide or control vehicular or pedestrian traffic at such places as streets, schools, railroad crossings, or construction sites.

Customs And Border Protection Officers

Investigate and inspect persons, common carriers, goods, and merchandise, arriving in or departing from country orbetween states to detect violations of immigration and customs laws and regulations.

Digital Forensics Analysts

Conduct investigations on computer-based crimes establishing documentary or physical evidence, such as digital media and logs associated with cyber intrusion incidents. Analyze digital evidence and investigate computer.

CHAPTER12

Careers in marketing and communication

1. Marketing Communications Specialist

Marketing communications specialists use their skills to help craft and manage an organization's message. The daily tasks associated with this role often include preparing marketing materials such as brochures, emails, press releases, newsletters, presentations, and other promotional messaging materials.

These professionals often have a balance of creative skills, and especially strong writing skills, as well as a strong knowledge of communication strategies. Employers typically search for job candidates who have at least a bachelor's degree in marketing communications or similar field and relevant work experience.

2. Social Media Specialist

Social media has become a powerful way for organizations to communicate and engage with their audiences. Organizations in a wide variety of fields now employ social media specialists who are charged with implementing marketing strategies and managing communications through social media platforms.

Although formal education may not be necessary to understand the different social media platforms, professionals in this role often hold a bachelor's degree in marketing, communications, or a related field. Having a strong educational background is essential to understanding the strategies that drive an organization's social media activities, as well as other key functions like reporting and analysis.

3. Public Relations Specialist

Similar to marketing communications specialists, public relations specialists are also focused on managing an organization's messaging, as well as ensuring that the public perception of the organization remains positive. Much of a PR professional's work is focused on executing marketing strategies. However, when the need arises, these professionals may work to defuse situations which may be seen in an unfavorable light.

Due to the complex nature of maintaining a brand's image, PR specialists often hold a bachelor's degree in a field like business or communications. Employers also look for candidates with experience in public relations.

5. Customer Relationship Manager

A customer relationship manager is typically charged with maintaining relationships with an organization's customers and clients. Within this role, the customer relationship manager effectively acts as the liaison between the organization and its clients in order to meet the needs of both parties and facilitate long-term working relationships.

Since this role is so focused on building strong relationships, these professionals must have excellent interpersonal and communication skills in addition to a strong knowledge of the business. As a result, most employers search for candidates with a degree in business, marketing, or similar field plus relevant experience.

6. Marketing Coordinator

Marketing coordinators are professionals who are skilled in developing and coordinating marketing campaigns for their organizations. Marketing coordinators must have strong written and verbal communication skills in order to carry out their roles effectively. They must be able to work with key stakeholders to understand the requirements for certain marketing efforts and present deliverables, as well as coordinate the efforts of others in the marketing department to facilitate projects.

A bachelor's degree in marketing communications or related field is typically the minimum requirement for securing a job as a marketing communications coordinator due to the skills and experience required for the role. Since this job does often require marketing experience, professionals often start with an entry-level position and aspire to reach this level.

7. Marketing Manager

Marketing managers are senior members of an organization's marketing departments who drive strategy and oversee marketing efforts. Similar to marketing coordinators, the title of marketing manager is one that professionals typically earn after several years of experience in the field.

The majority of those in this position have earned at least a bachelor's degree and have strong communication, management, and critical thinking skills as well as deep knowledge of marketing and communications strategy

CHAPTER 13

Careers in science, technology, engineering and math(STEM)

This career cluster is organized into two career pathways:

Engineering And Technology

Science and math

Careers include:

Biologist or microbiologist

Chemist

Biochemist or biophysicist

Mathematician

Statistician

Engineer: Aerospace, industrial, biotechnology, chemical, marine, materials, civil, petroleum

Engineering manager

Atmospheric or space scientist

Geoscientist or materials scientist

Surveying and mapping technician

Hydrologist

Architect

Naval architect

Architectural or civil drafter

Materials lab and supply technician

Quality technician

Nuclear equipment operation or monitoring technicians

Technical writer

Post-secondary education vocational teacher

CHAPTER 14

Careers in community and social services installation,rapair and maintenance

Emergency Management Directors

Emergency management directors prepare plans and procedures for responding to natural disasters or other emergencies. They also help lead the response during and after emergencies, often in coordination with public safety officials, elected officials, nonprofit organizations, and government agencies.

Health Educators And Community Health Workers

Health education specialists teach people about behaviors that promote wellness. They develop strategies to improve the well-being of individuals and communities. Community health workers advocate for residents' needs with healthcare providers and social service organizations. They implement wellness strategies by collecting data and discussing health concerns with members of specific populations.

Marriage And Family Therapists

Marriage and family therapists help people manage problems with their family and other relationships.

Probation Officers and Correctional Treatment Specialists

Probation officers and correctional treatment specialists provide social services to assist in rehabilitation of law offenders in custody or on probation or parole.

Rehabilitation Counselors

Rehabilitation counselors help people with physical, mental, developmental, or emotional disabilities live independently. They work with clients to overcome or manage the personal, social, or psychological effects of disabilities on employment or independent living.

School And Career Counselors And Advisors

School counselors help students develop academic and social skills and plans for after graduation. Career counselors and advisors help students and other clients develop skills, explore an occupation, or choose an educational program that will lead to a career.

Social And Community Service Managers

Social and community service managers coordinate and supervise social service programs and community organizations. They manage workers who provide social services to the public.

Social And Human Service Assistants

Social and human service assistants provide client services, including support for families, in a wide variety of fields, such as psychology, rehabilitation, and social work. They assist other workers, such as social workers, and they help clients find benefits or community services.

Social Workers

Social workers help people solve and cope with problems in their everyday lives. Clinical social workers also diagnose and treat mental, behavioral, and emotional issues.

Substance Abuse, Behavioral Disorder, And Mental Health Counselors

Substance abuse, behavioral disorder, and mental health counselors advise people who suffer from alcoholism, drug addiction, eating disorders, mental health issues, or other mental or behavioral problems. They provide treatment and support to help clients recover from addiction or modify problem behaviors.

Additional Community and Social Service Occupations

Clergy

Clergy conduct religious worship and perform other spiritual functions associated with beliefs and practices of religious faiths or denominations.

Counselors (All Other)

All counselors not listed separately.

Community And Social Service Specialists (All Other)

All community and social service specialists not listed separately.

Directors Of Religious Activities And Education

Directors of Religious Activities and Education plan, direct, or coordinate programs designed to promote the religious education or activities of a denominational group

CHAPTER 15

Passion as a driving tool in choosing the right career

Most times, People like to use the word passion interchangeably with words like determination, conviction, and love. Passion is a strong desire that can get you to do amazing things.

What Is Passion?

Passion is an emotion to be acted upon. Without action, passion yields no worthwhile results. Passion is the fuel in the fire of action. When you have passion for something, you love it even when you hate it.

A desire fueled by passion will bring about the greatest results in life.

I like to skateboard, but I don't have the determination to push myself through broken bones and hospital visits. That's why I'm not as good as I could be. I don't have a passion for it.

Passion can push you through difficult times because you don't care what it takes to become better. We all have the ability to create whatever kind of life we want. The secret to living the dream is hidden in our passions and what we do because of them.

How To Know What You're Passionate About?

Finding what you are passionate about is a journey in itself. Don't be frustrated if you don't feel like you know yet. Keep trying new things. It will come even if you have to build it. If you find your passion, or find yourself hot on its trail, don't give it up.

What if you know what you have a passion for but you don't do anything about it? This is the main problem with passion. You can have all the passion in the world for something but if you never do anything about it, that passion is useless.

Maybe you work a good job that pays all the bills but it doesn't allow you to truly follow your passion. You're afraid of what will happen if you change things up. Yes, change is scary, but it's not until we leave our comfort zone that we find what we've been missing out on.

You're the author of your life. Don't settle for the bare minimum just because it's working out right now.

You will never know what you're truly capable of unless you push yourself.

But even when you pursue your passion, you will find yourself tripped up by failures and other obstacles. You can't let that get to you. It happens to everyone on the path of following their passion. Abe Lincoln had a strong passion for building a great country. You think he let a few failures stop him from that? Don't let obstacles get you down.

14 Amazing Things That Happen

When You Live Your Passion

While society wants you to believe living your passion is irresponsible and foolish, we are going to focus on 14 amazing things that happens when you live your passion

1. Increased Self-Confidence

There is a little-known truth that everyone wants to be accepted for who they are. Yet, everyone is not comfortable expressing who they are. When you ignore the opinions of others and live your passion, you will become more comfortable expressing yourself.

Oftentimes, when you are not living your passion, you are living the life that you believe is acceptable to others. Your confidence will suffer when you give into the pressures of society, your friends, and family. This is largely because you are forcing yourself to do something that is of little interest to you.

There is probably a good reason for this, so when you are not working within your strengths and interests, your performance will be sub-par.

2. Lower Stress Levels

Job stress is the major source of stress for adults and it is associated with "increased rates of heart attack, hypertension and other disorders."[1]

Let me start out by debunking the misconception that all stress is bad. Those who follow their passions and those who do not will both encounter stress. The difference is in the kind of stress you come across.

Those who live their passion have an internal motivation that helps bring balance to their situation. As a result, they will most likely have stressful situations that come and go. A good example would be you have three important projects that need to be completed in the same day. Subsequently, you feel stressed until the day is over.

Those who are not living their passion are usually not enjoying their work and find it stressful every day. The act of waking up, putting their clothes on, and driving into work stresses them. They dread every Monday and yearn for every Friday.

3. Fulfillment In Your Work

As we started to touch on, there is nothing more draining than "working to live." You feel stuck because you have bills to pay and your job pays the bills.

Even though there is a bit of uncertainty surrounding your passion, you cannot underestimate the value of loving what you do.

By pursuing your passion, you will feel fulfilled in your work. You will no longer feel the need to listen to podcasts and audio-books while working (trying to fill that unfulfilled void). You will have the joy of living your passion, instead of planning to live your passion. There is nothing more rewarding than doing what you were called to do.

4. Mastery Of Work-Life Balance

There is a saying that if you live your passion, you no longer need a work-life balance. The premise is work-life balance is only needed when your work is draining.

When you are following your passion, your life is in constant balance. Your work does not feel like a job because you would do it for free.

Can you imagine, wishing you could be working because you truly enjoy what you do? Well, that is exactly what will happen when you are pursuing your passion.

5. Fewer Regrets Later In Life

In the end, most people will not regret the things they did, but things they did not do.

Imagine what your life would be like if you pursued all your dreams and passions. Now imagine if you ran into that person and had to explain to him why you did not pursue your passion. This is the real-life conversation most people are having when it is all but too late.

Take a risk and bet on yourself. Even if it does not work out exactly as you would have hoped, you will be better for it.

6. Personal Growth

The reason most people do not live their passion is because of the uncertainty surrounding their passion. You may have doubts regarding your ability to succeed financially, professionally, or even emotionally.

Sometimes, you are right to think this way. This does not mean you should accept this reality and do nothing about it. Instead, spend some time developing the skill-set needed to accomplish your passion.

You can become a rocket scientist if you still want to be an astronaut. You can practice and pursue your pilots license if you want still want to be a pilot.

Map out what skills you need to develop to live your passion and then take the steps to do so.

7. Positive Attraction

Sometimes you fear that your passion is not going to be received well by others. The thing about living a less than authentic life, you are going to attract the wrong people.

When you live your life and follow your passions, you are going to attract like-minded people.

To be honest, you are probably going to rub some people the wrong way when you are pursuing your passion. People do not like change and when you change, it could change your relationships.

Do not let this be something that will hold you back though. Your growth is tied to your willingness to pursue the beliefs that will enable you to achieve your goal.

8. Expand Your Comfort Zone

Do not fall into the trap of believing that you have to give everything up to follow your passion. These types of limiting beliefs keep most people from ever starting their journey to change their life.

In fact, you don't need to give up everything to start afresh

Allow yourself to slowly expand your comfort zone and try new things. You can continue to live your existing life, while pursuing new adventures on the side.

As you grow more comfortable in your ability to live your passion, you can slowly shift more time towards it. Before you know it, you will be all-in and living your life to the fullest.

9. Be Grateful

It is true that you can and should be grateful all the time. There is always something to be grateful for in your life. Even if you got a flat tire on you way home from work, at least you have a vehicle.

Similarly, you should always be grateful to have a job. Yet, there is little doubt that you will feel more grateful if you are doing something you are passionate about every day. You could realistically find yourself excited to wake up every morning because you know it is another day to fulfill your life's purpose.

10. Reconnect With Your Inner-Self

There was a time when you felt free. You felt like you could do anything and everything was possible.

When you start living your passion, you are most likely reconnecting with things you loved as a child. By taking a moment and realizing the things you loved before society told you what to love, you are finding a lost piece of yourself.

Revisit your childhood joys and take note of what you loved doing. Like me, you may find that you love putting puzzles together. This could speak on your analytical nature and help you understand why you are so passionate about putting things together and solving problems.

Whatever it may be, take a moment and rediscover the "real you" that was forced to "grow up".

11. Kinder Person

Your passion is most likely going to benefit a lot of people. There is something wrong with the world that you believe you can help improve. If more people would live their passion, there is little doubt the world would be a better place.

There is a peace and joy that you will find when you are living your passion, and that will rub off on your interactions with others. You may have heard the saying, "hurt people, hurt people". This means that the person who is bad at your job is most likely dealing with something in their own life.

When you pursue your passion, you are satisfied and at peace with the world, and you will be kinder to others.

12. Unleash Your Creativity

The thing about living a life absent of your passion is that you are most likely living the commonly walked path. Security in life is often the absence of creativity.

When you leave the path of least resistance and start to live your passion, you must unleash your creativity to succeed. You are going to be venturing into uncharted waters in your life and it can be intimidating. But that is where the magic happens.

When you find yourself face to face with an obstacle logged between you and your passion, you need to trust in yourself that you will prevail.

13. Change The Narrative

You have an inner voice that is telling you who you are, what you can do, and what you deserve. Sometimes you have split feelings about pursuing your passion. On the one hand, you are grateful for the life you have and content with everything it entails. Or you have a burning desire to pursue your passion and take a risk.

By understanding the limiting narrative you are telling yourself (I am not good enough, I should be happy with the job I have now, etc.), you will be better equipped to change your narrative.

Your new narrative will be grounded in an understanding that you can pursue your passion without that meaning you are ungrateful or unappreciative of the life you have now.

14. Conquer Your Fears

Fear leads to procrastination and procrastination leads to the death of your desire to pursue your passion.

Avoid the temptation to rationalize keeping things the way they are until you have more experience, more time, and more influence. There will always be something that could be better. If you give into your fears, they will only continue to grow.

By living your passion, you will have put your fears in their place. Remember, it is okay to be afraid, it is not okay to allow that fear to stall your efforts.

ABILITIES

What Are Abilities?

Abilities are commonly considered to be a special talent or skill to do something. You will hear this of prodigious talents a lot, "they had a natural ability". Ability is usually something you are born with and have been genetically blessed with. For example, a great swimmer like Michael Phelps had a huge genetic advantage over his competitors whilst he honed his skills with daily, hard practice to become the best swimmer the Olympics has ever seen.

It is the example above that sometimes muddies the water between skills and abilities. In essence they are related, they are designed to provide a specific function but they are different and it does matter.

Skills are what you can develop and harness. Ability is having something from birth that is harder to develop. In the example above, Phelps was genetically blessed with his height and feet size (perfect for a swimmer) but also more subtle and important things like his torso measurement, lung capacity and lactic acid threshold. His skills were to improve his strokes, his timing, his turns, his racecraft.

Another way of looking at ability is that, what an ability means is that you have the capacity to do something. A skill on the other hand is being able to do something well. I.e. Michael is a natural born swimmer, but he became a champion by working at it.

Examples of ability

Here are some examples of ability that apply to the above definitions:

Research

How we find information, collect, analyse and interpret it.

Problem solving

How we handle challenges and find solutions in difficult moments.

Art

How we create art in any form. From photography to drawing or sculpting.

Craft

How we use our manual abilities to create something from very little or sometimes nothing.

Public speaking

The talent of effectively addressing a room - some people naturally have this from the first day of their lives.

Negotiation

How to effectively communicate between two parties that have differing views to see a common ground.

11 ABILITIES THAT EXIST

1:Musical abilities

2: Natural abilities

3: Movement abilities

4: Interpersonal abilities

5: Intrapersonal abilities

6: Logical abilities

7: Linguistic abilities

8: Digital abilities

9: Visual abilities

10: Teaching abilities

11: Spiritual Abilities

1:Musical abilities:Musical ability as a term is used to describe the sensitivity for music, the ability to understand music, and/or the ability to produce music. There is no standard definition, and it is hard to measure musical ability. One can only measure how well a person can perceive musical stimuli such as small changes in pitch, loudness, rhythm, and other sub-domains of music processing. It is generally accepted that some people show higher musical ability than others.

Possible careers for those with musical abilities include:

Singer,songwriters,music producers, music arrangers etc

12:Natural Abilities:

People who have natural abilities often enjoy spending time in nature,love plants and animals and they understand how different compounds and elements in the world interact with each other.

They have an act for survival skills,they can identify individual plants and species, understand how animals behave and they know how everything in nature is connected.

Possible careers for these set of people include:

Food scientist,foresters, wildlife management,soil scientist including medicine and other medical related courses because everything in our body has to do with nature

13.Movement Abilities:

people who have movement abilities tend to love moving their bodies,whether large explosive movement or the tiniest form of movement,they just want to move their body.

The have the powerful ability to control every muscle in their body, allowing them to do amazing things that are often referred to being impossible for the average person.

Possible careers for people who possess movement abilities include:

Dance,sports,fine craftsmanship, personal trainer and marshall art etc

14: Interpersonal Ability:

People who have affinity for this have a deep understanding about relationship between people,they could quickly read someone's body language and get an idea of how they are feeling,and they are usually good in holding conversation,they understand human nature and help people interact with each other.

Possible career opportunities include:

sales, content creation,event planning, relationship counseling and even working in law enforcement.

15. Intrapersonal Ability:

People who have affinity for this have a deep understanding of themselves,they know how to look in the mirror to spot what needs to work, allowing them to reflect and adjust.This is an extremely powerful ability that is crucial for self improvement because the only way you can improve is if you can identify what you need to work on,on the first place.

Possible career paths include:

therapist,self improvement coaches, motivational speakers.

16. Logical Ability:

People who fall under this category can reason well,they may have some interesting ability in the sciences,most importantly,they are interested in the TRUTH,they act on feeling more than emotion.

> ***Possible career paths include investors, scientist,inventors and entrepreneurs.***

17. Linguistic Ability:

People who excel in this have a Deep understanding of their language and the emotions that comes with certain words,they are usually articulated,and usually have vast vocabulary,they typically enjoy reading and listening to great speakers,most importantly,they know how to craft messages in an engaging way making them more influencial than the average person.

> ***possible careers include:***

writer,speaker,poet, copywriter and translator.

18. Digital Ability:

This is one of the newest abilities, because the digital world is dominating in the last decades,most people who fall into this category are the younger generations as growing up in the digital world had a major impact on them,they have a deep understanding of how the digital world works, social media,SEO, digital marketing,memes going viral are all things that fall under this category.

Possible careers include

digital marketing, vlogging etc

19. Visual Ability:

People who have this ability have a deep appreciation for the aesthetics,this means,they can spot what looks pleasant to the eye,they can tell which color combination and what shape looks good, they can also visualize and imagine complex images in their head,often allowing them to recreate this images on paper.

Possible careers include

architect,illustrators,animators, fashion designers and graphics designers.

20. Teaching:

People gifted with this ability takes complicated subjects and deliver them in such a clear way that even young kids can understand,they can spot what someone is doing right or wrong for the field that they specialize in and most importantly,they gain a deep sense of satisfaction seeing their students grow .

Possible career include:

teaching, consulting, creating educational contents and even parenting

21. Spiritual Ability:

This is a very unique category as it's something almost everyone gets interested in as they age, because it's the ability to think about bigger question in life,like questions about the Afterlife,the meaning of life,is there God.

Career opportunities include

philosophers, pastors,monks etc

RELATIONSHIP BETWEEN PASSION AND ABILITY

Passion, Ability And Careers

Let's take a closer look at the relationship between passion and ability and how it impacts careers.

I will be giving four examples to enumerate my point

1:HIGH PASSION+LOW ABILITY=FRUSTRATED TALENT

2:HIGH PASSION+HIGH ABILITY=THE SWEET SPOT

3: LOW PASSION+LOW ABILITY=THE BAD PLACE

4:LOW PASSION+HIGH ABILITY=WASTED TALENT

Each of the four things in the Passion and Ability example describes a state you are in at that moment in terms of your ability and passion for a specific role.

So which is more vital - Passion or Ability? That's like asking which is more important - the engine or the steering wheel. You need both. And the same applies to Passion and Ability. You can swim super fast - that's Ability. And if you have Passion, then the chance of catching up

Passion, Ability And Careers

Let's take a closer look at the relationship between passion and ability and how it impacts careers.

Each of the four Quadrants in the Passion and Ability Matrix describes a state you are in at that moment in terms of your ability and passion for a specific role.

> ***Example 1- The Frustrated Talent: High Passion + Low Ability.***

Neil Armstrong dreamed of walking on the moon. But before he took a giant leap for mankind he made many smaller steps first – flew on the Gemini 8 mission, studied aeronautical engineering, served as a test pilot and was an Eagle Scout!

Skip the small steps and you miss the lessons you are supposed to learn and deprive self of the skills you need to fulfil your passion. But if you dedicate yourself and lay it down brick by brick you can achieve almost anything.

And if you hit a roadblock look to Colonel Saunders of KFC. After an assortment of mediocre career choices, he started selling his chicken recipe at 65 years old. Apparently, he failed 1009 times before making his first sale. In other words, he had 1009 tries to get really good at selling.

When you have passion, Keeping At It becomes easier. Then ability will follow. And this move you to example 2 - the Sweet Spot!

Example 2: The Sweet Spot: High Passion + High Ability.

This is where most want to be - love what you do and great at doing it.

Ironically the sweet spot is also a place where Passion can diminish and Ability stagnate.

An IT Director loved his job and everybody praised his ability. So he stopped bringing his 'A' game because even at a lower gear he was killing it. But if you are not keeping at it, then you are falling behind. Over time his passion and ability dipped and career trajectory shifted from going upward to how to keep his job.

There is an antidote - Keep Moving - to different roles with new, challenging work.

Example 3: The Bad Place: Low Passion + Low Ability.

You have little interest in your job and are bad at it. A vicious cycle of failure starts and the impact of each failure is compounded - confidence is battered, self-belief stripped and going to work is like going to prison.

But it's never too late to break the cycle.

A salesperson performed badly until he was redeployed to a customer service role. He did well. Though he took a salary cut, he was never happier. He stopped being afraid of failing and started rebuilding his ability to perform. The more he improves. the more he loves his job!

Remember you are not a hostage of the examples mentioned above! Ask for help, coaching, training to improve ability or get deployed to another role which leverages your strength or sparks passion or both. These will move you out of the bad place and into a different quadrant.

Q 4: Wasted Talent: Low Passion + High Ability.

Work in this quadrant pays the rent but offers little to the soul.

Andre Agassi, the tennis champion lost his passion for the game even though he continued winning titles. The pressure of winning dominated everything including his life.

A different example. A friend became a doctor to please his parents. The cool piece of his story is over the years, he got really good at his profession and discovered his gift - his ability to gain trust - people put their lives in his hands. This changed everything. "I do zero work because I am too busy caring for my patients."

Yes, high ability can influence passion positively. But if your passion remains low, two things can happen. You will always be competent so long as you keep learning your craft. Then if you need it, seek an outlet outside of work to fulfil a passion. Another scenario is your lack of interest ultimately impacts your ability. Practising and learning get tougher and atrophy sets in. Eventually, you move into Q3: the Bad Place - low passion, low ability.

Lessons

Keep Moving. Ironically you are at your most vulnerable when you make it to the top because you do what most everyone does- enjoy the view. It's healthy to take a break but also tempting to make the Comfort Zone your final destination. Keep Moving at a sustainable pace to new and challenging assignments.

Keep At It. Yale professor, Amy Wrzesniewski discovered that the strongest predictor of seeing work as a calling was the number of years spent on the job. The longer you do the job, the better you get, the more likely you'll love it.

When to Keep Moving and when to Keep At it? Keep Moving when the job gets too easy or when you stop having fun. Keep At it when you haven't tried your best or you need more time to improve ability and get the results

Slowing down is the enemy of Passion and Ability. It can happen when you are at the top of your game and when you are down but giving up. The great ones never stop moving. So if fulfilling your potential means the world to you, then take a break when you need it, and then Keep Moving. Keep At It.

CHAPTER 16

How to choose your career

With thousands of options, how will you choose a career that's right for you? If you don't have any idea what you want to do, the task may seem insurmountable. Fortunately, it isn't. Follow an organized process and you will increase your chances of making a good decision.

Assess Yourself

Before you can choose the right career, you must learn about yourself. Your values, interests, soft skills, and aptitudes, in combination with your personality type, make some occupations a good fit for you, and others completely inappropriate.

Use self-assessment tools, and career tests to gather information about your traits and, subsequently, generate a list of occupations that are a good fit based on them. Some people choose to work with a career counselor or other career development professionals who can help them navigate this process.

How To Use Self Assessment Tools To Choose A Career

Individuals who are trying to choose a career often wonder if they can take a test that can tell them what occupation is right for them. Unfortunately, there isn't a single test that will magically tell you what to do with the rest of your life. A combination of self-assessment tools, however, will help with the decision.

During the self-assessment phase of the career planning process, gather information about yourself to make an informed decision. A self-assessment should include thoroughly examining your values, interests, personality, and aptitude.

Values: the things that are important, like achievement, status, and autonomy

Interests: what you enjoy doing, i.e., playing golf, taking long walks, and hanging out with friends

Personality: a person's traits, motivational drives, needs, and attitudes

Aptitude: the activities you are good at, such as writing, computer programming, and teaching. They may be natural skills or ones acquired through training and education.

Many people hire a career counselor to help them with this process and administer a variety of self-assessment inventories. What follows is a discussion of the different types of tools, as well as some other things to consider when using your results to choose a career.

Value Inventories

Your values are possibly the most important thing to consider when choosing an occupation. If you don't take them into account when planning your career, there's a good chance you'll dislike your work and therefore not succeed in it. For example, someone who prefers autonomy would not be happy in a job where he or she can't be independent.

There are two types of values: intrinsic and extrinsic. Intrinsic values are related to the work itself and what it contributes to society. Extrinsic values include external features, such as physical setting and earning potential. Value inventories will ask questions like the following:

Is a high salary important to you?

Is it important for your work to involve interacting with people?

Is it important for your work to contribute to society?

Is having a prestigious job important to you?

During a self-assessment, a career counselor may administer one of the following value inventories: Minnesota Importance Questionnaire (MIQ), Survey of Interpersonal Values (SIV), or Temperament and Values Inventory (TVI).

Interest Inventories

Career development professionals also frequently administer interest inventories such as the Strong Interest Inventory (SII), formerly called the Strong-Campbell Interest Inventory. These self assessment tools ask individuals to answer a series of questions regarding their (surprise) interests. E.K. Strong, a psychologist, pioneered their development. He found, through data he gathered about people's likes and dislikes of a variety of activities, objects, and types of persons, that people in the same career (and satisfied in that career) had similar interests.

Dr. John Holland and others provided a system of matching

interests with one or more of six types: realistic, investigative, artistic, social, enterprising and conventional. He then matched these types with occupations. When you take an interest inventory, the results are compared with this study to see where you fit in—are your interests similar to those of a police officer or to those of an accountant, for example?

Personality Inventories

Many personality inventories used in career planning are based on Psychiatrist Carl Jung's personality theory. He believed four pairs of opposite preferences—the way individuals choose to do things— make up people's personalities. They are extroversion and introversion (how one energizes), sensing and intuition (how one perceives information), thinking or feeling (how one makes decisions), and judging and perceiving (how one lives his or her life). One preference from each pair makes up an individual's personality type.

Career counselors often use results from assessments based on Jungian Personality Theory, such as the Myers-Briggs Type Indicator (MBTI), to help clients choose careers. They believe individuals with a particular personality type are better suited to specific occupations. An example would be that an introvert would not do well in a career that requires him or her to be around other people all the time.

Aptitude Assessments

When deciding what field to enter, you need to discover your aptitudes. An aptitude is a natural or acquired ability. In addition to looking at what you are good at doing, also consider what you enjoy. It is possible to be quite adept at a particular skill, yet despise every second spent using it. Generally speaking, though, people usually enjoy what they are good at.

While you're assessing your skills, think about the time you are willing to spend to acquire more advanced or new skills. A question to ask yourself is this—if a career holds all the qualities I find appealing but it takes X years to prepare for it, would I be willing and able to make this time commitment?

Additional Things to Consider

While going through the self-assessment process, take into account other factors that will influence your career choice. For example, think about your family responsibilities and your ability to pay for education or training. Don't forget that self-assessment is the first step in the career planning process, not the last.

After completing this phase, go on to the next one, career exploration. With your self-assessment results in mind, next, evaluate a variety of occupations to see which ones are the best fit. While your self-assessment may indicate a particular career is suitable for someone with your interests, personality, values, and aptitude, it doesn't mean it is the one that is most right for you. Similarly, don't discount an occupation just because it doesn't show up in the results of a self-assessment. Do a lot of research about any profession in which you are interested.

Make A List Of Careers To Explore

You probably have multiple lists of occupations in front of you at this point—one generated by each of the self-assessment tools you used. To keep yourself organized, you should combine them into one master list.

First, look for careers that appear on multiple lists and copy them onto a blank page. Title it "Occupations to Explore."

If your self-assessments indicated a career is a good fit for you based on several of your traits, it's worth exploring.

Next, find any occupations on your lists that appeal to you. They may be careers you know a bit about and want to explore further. Also, include professions about which you don't know much. You might learn something unexpected.

Explore The Careers On Your List

At this point, you'll be thrilled you managed to narrow your list down to only 10 to 20 options. Now you can get some basic information about each of the occupations on your list.

Find job descriptions and educational, training, and licensing requirements in published sources. Learn about advancement opportunities. Use government-produced labor market information to get data about earnings and job outlook.

For example, the Bureau of Labor Statistics publishes "Career Outlook" analysis articles for many professions. These articles supplement the "Occupational Outlook Handbook" which also offers detailed statistics on career pay, growth trends, and more.1

Career exploration

exploration is the second stage of the career planning process. During the first stage, a self-assessment, you learn about your personality, interests, aptitudes, and values. After using various tools to gather this information, you are left with a list of careers that are a good fit for someone with traits similar to yours.

Although the careers on your list appear to be suitable, it does not mean you can just go ahead and randomly choose any one of them. There are other things to consider. Each occupation has characteristics that will make it a better idea to choose some over others.

Since you can only have one career at a time, your goal, after learning about all the careers that might be a good fit for you, is to eventually have one remaining that is the BEST fit. Try not to eliminate any profession from your list until you do some research, even if you think you know something about it. You may be surprised by what you learn when you dig for information. If you cross a career off your list because of some preconceived notion, you could end up eliminating one of your best options.

Start With The Basics

At first, you will just want to gather some basic information about each occupation on your list. Let's assume you have a list of ten careers. Before spending a lot of time on in-depth research, do some preliminary fact-finding that will allow you to narrow down your list. It will include looking at a job description and labor market information, including job outlook, median salary and educational and training requirements.

The Occupational Outlook Handbook, published by the U.S. Bureau of Labor Statistics, a government agency, does a good job of presenting basic career information. Another useful resource is the O*Net Database, sponsored by the US Department of Labor/ Employment and Training Administration (USDOL/ETA) through a grant to the North Carolina Department of Commerce. You can also read individual career profiles or delve into careers by field.

After learning about all the occupations on your list, you will find that several of them don't appeal to you. It could be for a variety of reasons. For example, you may decide that you wouldn't enjoy the job duties of a particular occupation or that you can't or don't want to meet the educational and training requirements. The earnings may be lower than you thought they would be or the job outlook tells you that employment opportunities will be poor. After completing your preliminary research, you will be left with a list that contains between three and five careers on it.

Delve Deeper

After you narrow down your list of career choices, your research should become more involved. You will want to learn what working in the field is really like before you actually work in it. The best way to do this is to talk to people who do.

Figure out who, in your professional network, knows people who work in the field or fields in which you are interested, or ask around to see if any of them have contacts who do.

Set up informational interviews with anyone who has experience working in the careers you are considering. Those whose experience is more recent make better subjects.

See if any of those people are willing to let you shadow him or her on the job for a day or two.

Consider doing an internship to learn about a work field and get experience.

After you complete your in-depth research, you should be able to determine which career is a good match for you. Try not to get too frustrated if you can't make a decision by this point. You may not have enough information yet. Continue to do more research until you can comfortably choose the best career for you.

Create A "Short List"

Now you have more information, start to narrow down your list even further. Based on what you learned from your research so far, begin eliminating the careers you don't want to pursue any further. You should end up with two to five occupations on your "short list."

If your reasons for finding a career unacceptable are non-negotiable, cross it off your list. Remove everything with duties that don't appeal to you. Eliminate careers that have weak job outlooks. Get rid of any occupation if you are unable or unwilling to fulfill the educational or other requirements, or if you lack some of the soft skills necessary to succeed in it.

Things to Know About Job Outlook

What It Is It and How Can You Use It to Help You Choose a Career

Job outlook is a forecast of the change in the number of people employed in a particular occupation over a set period, for example, two years, five years or ten years. Economists at the Bureau of Labor Statistics (BLS), a division of the United States Department of Labor, predict whether—and by how much—the rate of employment will increase or decrease between a base year and a target year. The BLS publishes this information for hundreds of occupations in the Occupational Outlook Handbook and updates it every two years.

The BLS compares an occupation's projected employment change, usually over 10 years, to the average projected change in employment for all occupations over the same period. They describe a career's projected job outlook by saying it will:

Grow much faster than average (an increase of 14% or more)

Grow faster than average (an increase of between 9% and 13%)

Grow about as fast as average (an increase of between 5% to 8%)

Grow more slowly than average (an increase of between 2% and 4%)

Have little or no change (a decrease or increase of 1% or less)

Decline (a decrease of at least 2%)

Why You Must Consider Job Outlook When Choosing a Career

It is essential to consider an occupation's employment outlook, among other labor market information, when you are choosing a career. After determining a career is a good fit based on the results of a self-assessment, take the time to learn everything about it before investing money and time preparing for it. That must include determining whether you are likely to find a job when your training and education are complete. While there are no guarantees even for occupations with an exceptional outlook, the odds should be in your favor.

Also, investigate the job outlook for your current occupation when you are thinking about changing careers. One of the reasons to make a career change is a worsening job outlook. If employment opportunities are few and it looks like they will get even worse, it may be time to prepare to work in a different field.

Limitations Of Job Outlook Figures

While it is important to find out whether an occupation has a positive job outlook, this projection alone does not give you all the required information to know about your chances of finding future employment. Look at job prospects as well. The same economists who estimate employment growth also compare the number of job seekers with the number of job openings to determine job prospects. Although the BLS may project employment in a particular occupation will grow much faster than average over the next 10 years, the number of available jobs may be few.

One reason may be that some fields don't employ many people. Even if economists expect high growth, it may not translate into a significant number of opportunities for those hoping to enter a field or industry.

Another important thing to keep in mind is that, despite economists' ability to make educated predictions, job outlook and prospects can change unexpectedly. Employment growth can slow down, and it can speed up, due to the influence of a variety of factors. For example, if more job candidates are available than there are job openings, it will be harder to find work. Likewise, when there are fewer qualified applicants, it will be easier to get hired. Additionally, a downturn or upturn in an industry will change the outlook.

While looking at national data is an essential first step in researching the job outlook for an occupation, don't skip also investigating the forecasts for that occupation in the state in which you want to work. Use Projections Central: State Occupational Projections to find long- and short-term occupational predictions that will also affect your ability to get a job.

Conduct Informational Interviews

When you have only a few occupations left on your list, start doing more in-depth research. Arrange to meet with people who work in the occupations in which you are interested. They can provide firsthand knowledge about the careers on your short list.

Access your network, including LinkedIn, to find people with whom to have these informational interviews.

Make Your Career Choice

Finally, after doing all your research, you are probably ready to make your choice. Pick the occupation that you think will bring you the most satisfaction based on all the information you have gathered. Realize that you are allowed do-overs if you change your mind about your choice at any point in your life. Many people change their careers at least a few times.

Identify Your Goals

Once you make a decision, identify your long- and short-term goals. This helps to chart a course toward eventually landing work in your chosen field. Long-term goals typically take about three to five years to reach, while you can usually fulfill a short-term goal in six months to three years.

Let the research you did about required education and training be your guide. If you don't have all the details, do some more research. Once you have all the information you need, set your goals.

An example of a long-term goal would be completing your education and training. Short-term goals include applying to college, apprenticeships, other training programs, and internships.

How To Set Short- and Long-Term Career Goals

You may feel setting long-term and short-term goals is a waste of time. But goal setting is an important part of the career planning process. Increase your chances of reaching your short- and long-term goals by making them measurable, realistic, and more. Not planning for your future can make for a chaotic one

How Goals Can Impact Your Career Success

Setting goals is a significant component of the career planning process. To have a successful and satisfying career, define your goals and devise a strategy to achieve them. A roadmap that will take you from choosing an occupation to working and succeeding at it is called a career action plan.1

Your career action plan must have both long- and short-term goals. It is imperative to include the steps you need to take to reach each one, along with ways to overcome challenges that might get in your way

Note:Since career plans and goals, even very well-thought-out ones, don't always work out, it is essential to include alternatives that you can implement when the need arises

Short-Term Goals Vs. Long-Term Goals

Short term goals are accomplished in 6-36 months while long term goals are accomplished in 3-5 years

Daily or weekly tasks can help you achieve your short-term goal while Short-term goals are necessary to achieve the long-term goal

Goals are broadly classified into two categories: short-term goals and long-term goals. You will be able to accomplish a short-term goal in approximately six months to three years, while it will usually take three to five years to reach a long-term one. Sometimes you can achieve a short-term goal in fewer than three months and a long-term one may take more than five years to complete.

To achieve each long-term goal, you must first accomplish a series of both short-term goals and additional long-term goals. For example, let's say you aspire to become a doctor. That may be your ultimate long-term goal, but before you can tackle it, you must achieve a few others like completing college (four years), medical school (another four years), and a medical residency (three to eight years).

Along the road to reaching those long-term goals, there are several short-term goals to clear first. They include excelling in entrance exams and applying to college, medical school, and eventually residencies. Since grades matter when it comes to achieving those goals, it is necessary to break your short-term goals down even further, like earning a high-grade point average.

Short-term goals require you to take action every day or every week. For example, if you want to get a new job, you may need to update your resume, scan job boards frequently, and send applications on a weekly basis.

Setting Short- and Long-Term Goals You Can Achieve

Your hard work will play the most prominent role in your success, but if you don't formulate your goals correctly, it will be much more challenging to accomplish them. Your short-term and long-term goals must meet the following criteria:

Make your goals specific: You might say, "I want to be successful." Well, who doesn't? But can you define what success means? Success to one person may mean becoming the CEO of a company while to another person it may mean getting home from work by 6 p.m. every day.

Your goals must be measurable: Have a timeframe for achieving your goals and a way to determine when you have reached them. You can even break them down into smaller milestones that you can measure along the way.

Don't be negative: Your goal should be something you want rather than something you want to avoid. It is much better to say, for instance, "I want to improve my skills over the next four years so that I qualify for a better job" than "I don't want to be stuck in this job for another four years."

Be realistic: Your long-term goals must be compatible with your abilities and skills. Stating "I want to win a Grammy Award" if you can't sing or play an instrument may not be the right goal for you. Consider your skills and set goals that make sense for your experience.

Take small steps over time to achieve your goal by the deadline: You don't have to have a deadline for your goal, but it may help you stay on track to reach it. Break a long-term goal down into smaller goals. It is better to take baby steps than one big giant leap.

your ultimate long-term goal, but before you can tackle it, you must achieve a few others like completing college (four years), medical school (another four years), and a medical residency (three to eight years).

Short-term goals require you to take action every day or every week. For example, if you want to get a new job, you may need to update your resume, scan job boards frequently, and send applications on a weekly basis.

Pair each goal with an action: For instance, if your goal is to write a book, sign up for a book writing seminar or practice writing one chapter per week for one month.

Be flexible: Don't give up if you encounter obstacles that threaten your progress. Instead, modify your goals accordingly. Let's say you need to continue working to make money, but that it will keep you from going to college full-time. Although it may not be possible to finish your bachelor's degree in four years, you can enroll in school part-time and finish in six or eight years instead. Flexibility also means being willing to let go of goals that are no longer meaningful and instead put your energy into pursuing other ones.

Note:As you progress in your career, your goals may change—and that's OK. Take time to assess your career, education, experience, and skills every six months or year so you can reprioritize your goals that you want to achieve.

Write a Career Action Plan

Put together a career action plan, a written document that lays out all the steps you will have to take to reach your goals. Think of it as a road map that will take you from point A to B, then to C and D. Write down all your short- and long-term goals and the steps you will have to take to reach each one. Include any anticipated barriers that could get in the way of achieving your goals—and the ways you can overcome them.

This may sound like a lot of work—and it is. But it's much easier to forge a career path when you know what you want. Taking these steps early will save you a lot of struggle and uncertainty in the long run.

Writing A Career Action Plan

Developing a career action plan is the fourth step in the career planning process. You should write one after doing a thorough self-assessment, a complete exploration of viable career options, and determining which one is the best match. Next comes the action plan.

A career action plan is like road map that will get you from point A—choosing an occupation—to Point B—becoming employed in that career. It even helps you get past Point B, to Points C through Z, as your career advances. It is also referred to as an Individualized (or Individual) Career Plan or an Individualized (or Individual) Career Development Plan.

Background Information

Create a worksheet you can use to outline your career action plan. It should contain the four sections below.

Employment History/Education And Training

Title the first section of your worksheet "Employment History/ Education and Training." This part is straightforward. List any jobs you've had in reverse chronological order, from most recent to least recent. Include the location of the company, your job title, and the dates you worked at that job.

When you eventually write your resume, having organized this information will prove very helpful. That goes for the next part as well—Education and Training. List the schools you attended, the dates you attended them, and the credits, certificates, or degrees you earned. Also list additional training and any professional licenses you hold.

Next, list volunteer or other unpaid experience. You may find that several of these activities are relevant to your occupational goals.

By volunteering, you may have developed skills that will play a vital role your future career. Again, you can use this information on your resume, on job interviews, or when you apply to college or graduate school.

Self Assessment Results

The next section of your worksheet should be "Self Assessment Results." If you met with a career counselor or similarly trained professional who conducted a self-assessment to help you gather information about yourself, this is where you can write down the results you got from them, including the occupations that were suggested to you during that phase. You may even want to attach the information you gathered when you explored these careers so you can refer to your notes later on.

Out of all the occupations you explored, at some point in the process, you narrowed your choices down to one of them. That is the one you plan to pursue. You may even have two occupations—one to aim for in the short term and one to strive for in the long term. For example, you can say you want to become a nurse's aid first, and then after you get some experience, you plan to become a registered nurse.

Short-Term And Long-Term Goals

The next section should be a place for you to list your occupational and educational goals. They should correspond to one another since reaching your occupational goals will usually be dependent upon reaching your educational ones. You should have short-term goals—those you can reach in a year or less—and long-term goals that you can reach in five or fewer years. You can use increments of one or two years in this five-year plan as well. This breakdown will make your plan easier to follow.

If your long-term occupational goal is to become a lawyer, here's what your short-term and long-term plans might look like:

Year One: Complete my bachelor's degree (12 credits left to go), apply to law school, get accepted to law school

Year Two through Year Four: Enter law school, study hard and earn good grades, graduate from law school with many job offers

Year Five: Begin working in a law firm

Barriers to Reaching Goals

As you try to reach your goals, you may face some barriers. You will have to find ways to get around them. In this section of your action plan, you can list anything that may get in the way of being able to reach your goals. Then list possible ways to overcome them.

For example, you may be the primary caregiver for your children or elderly parents, which may interfere with your ability to complete your degree. You can deal with this barrier by enlisting the help of your spouse or another relative. Perhaps you can arrange for child or adult day care.

Key Takeaways

To find the best career fit, you must first assess yourself and make a list of careers you think might match your interests and skills.

After researching those careers, narrow down your selection to a "short list" of career fields to explore further with informational interviews.

Once you're ready, you can pick a career field, set goals, and create an action plan to achieve those goals.

You're On Your Way

A well-thought-out career action plan will prove to be a very useful tool. You've gone through the career planning process carefully, choosing a suitable occupation. Setting goals and planning what you need to do to realize them will ensure that you reach your career destination.

CHAPTER 17

Why people choose the wrong careers

It seems we can do two things to improve our lot: reduce the amount of time spent working, or improve our satisfaction with our work.

Assuming we can't work less, let's find something more enjoyable to do.

Seems easy enough. Why is it so hard?

Reason 1: You Don't Know Yourself

When I was living in school I recall a conversation with a good friend about self-awareness. I was in the middle of one of my self-discovery experiments, this time attempting to write down every thought that entered my head over the course of a week.

The results were conclusive: I'm crazy.

My wise friend offered his advice: "If you want to get to know yourself, just look around your apartment. What kind of person lives there? What books does he have on his shelf? What photos does he have up on the wall?"

It's often the simplest advice that hits hardest.

Billionaire "Shark Tank" star Mark Cuban has shared that "self-awareness is one of the most important skills for any professional."

The problem is that we're never taught how to be self-aware. Understanding ourselves takes a back seat to understanding Algebra and Economics, so we have to put in the work to make up for lost ground.

Get to know yourself.

Play detective.

Look around your home: what kind of person lives there? What do they like, read, watch? What matters to them?

Last week I made a list of all the times this month that I was "in the zone": so engaged in what I was doing that I completely lost track of time. I noticed that a large percentage of those times was when I was creating something.

Like writing.

That's a clue.

Keep picking up clues, write them down. See what kind of picture emerges.

Reason 2: Social Pressure Will Get To You

There's a famous psychology experiment that clearly shows how and why social pressure will get to you, if it hasn't already.

Ten people in a room were given the below two cards and told to state out loud which comparison line (A, B or C) was most like the target line. The answer was always obvious, and the "test participant" sat at the end of the row and gave his or her answer last.

The number of times each participant conformed to the majority view was measured.

How do you think the participants fared?

On average, about one third (32%) of the participants who were placed in this situation went along and conformed with the clearly incorrect majority.

What does this mean for our careers?

I think it means that knowing ourselves and where we want to go isn't enough. We have to be ruthlessly courageous in protecting those dreams from the tyranny of the majority.

What happens when you know you want to do "C" in your career but everyone around you thinks "A" is a better choice?

What happens when you know you want to do "C" in your career but everyone around you is doing "B?"

The first decision you have to make before you choose your career is to choose who it is that's going to do the choosing.

It's great to get input from books, mentors, family, but try balancing that with silent time by yourself to do your own reflection.

> ***Or just do what everyone else does.***

"You enter the forest at the darkest point, where there is no path. Where there is a way or path, it is someone else's path." -- Joseph Campbell

Reason 3: You're Asking The Wrong Questions

Before my last career transition I found myself asking what, where, and how much, when I should've been asking who and why.

You'll be spending more time with the people in your office than with your own family.

> ***The who matters.***

> ***Who do you want to spend your life with?***

Instead of making a pro/cons list centered around your job title and duties, make a list of the traits you want in your boss and colleagues.

The why also matters.

In my previous life as an Executive Recruiter I interviewed and coached over 2000+ leaders at some of the best companies in the world, and one thing I noticed early on was that every time one of them lost sight of their "why" they came looking for a job change.

They had taken a role for the what, where, and how much, and after a few months or years came to realize that they weren't happy because they were missing a "why."

Startwithwhy.com.

Reason 4: Your Lens Is Too Narrow

In a recent career conversation with a sales personnel,she asked, "Should I stay in sales or go into marketing?"

Well those are two options.

I answered her question with a question, "Forget about sales vs marketing for a second. What would you do if anything was possible and you knew you couldn't fail?"

"Hmm, I don't know. I've never thought about that."

If you're thinking of making a change, open up a broader set of possibilities. There are endless ways to spend our working lives. Be creative, get them all out there. Start by listing 10 possible jobs you'd enjoy.

Forget that you're already 5-10 years down one path. It's never too late to re-align.

Reason 5: Your Goal Is Retirement

Tell me if you've ever heard someone say the following: "If I could just save XXX dollars, then I'd be able to quit and start doing what it is I really want to do."

Tell me if you've ever heard yourself say that.

What does it say about a working society when the main goal of working is to get to a state of not-working?

"This spending of the best part of one's life earning money in order to enjoy a questionable liberty during the least valuable part of it, reminds me of the Englishman who went to India to make a fortune first, in order that he might return to England and live the life of a poet." -- Henry David Thoreau

The risk of focusing too much on getting to retirement is that you're likely to let salary sway your career decisions.

If the end goal is retirement then the fastest means to get there would surely be the highest paying jobs, regardless of how much you enjoy them.

Which still puts us back here:

(A lot of time doing something) x (Not enjoying doing that something) = L

It seems to me that there's something much better than retirement. It's called doing work that you inherently enjoy.

(A lot of time doing something) x (Really enjoying doing that something) = L

So the next time you hear someone dreaming of retirement, tell them the good news: there's something better than retirement.

Reason 6:Parental Influence

"My dad wants me to be a doctor"

Most person's are stuck in there,not minding what they truly want but sticking what there parents want for them,some times,these parents are right but most times the create this unfulfillment in the life young person.you end up living your parents dream not your dreams

CHAPTER 18

What to do if you chose the wrong career

Realizing you're in the wrong career can be a tough pill to swallow.

The typical reaction usually includes a mix of panic, desperation, and discouragement. Those four (or more) years of school? A complete waste. The internships and entry-level positions that helped you get your foot in the door? Meaningless. All that time and talent spent on a career you've now determined that you absolutely hate

But it doesn't have to be that way. When you first realize that you may want to make a career

try to avoid the following common reactions—and learn to look at the situation in a different (and more positive) light.

1. Jumping To The Worst-Case Scenario

You've realized you're unhappy at work: You dread coming into the office each day, and you count down the minutes until the clock hits 5 PM. Immediately, you assume that to be happy, you need to make a major career switch—say, from designing healthcare software to running your own cupcake bakery.

Instead: Check Yourself

Take a step back. Before you start plotting your transition from software engineer to pastry chef extraordinaire, take some time to figure out if it's truly your career that you don't enjoy—or simply your current job environment.

Maybe you enjoy the basic job functions of your role, but you can't stand the majority of your co-workers or your micromanaging boss, who's hindering your career advancement. Perhaps you don't enjoy developing software for the banking industry, but would be much more motivated to perform the same role for a nonprofit with a mission you could stand behind.

Try to pinpoint the exact reason for your discontent. If it's something that could be remedied by taking a similar role in a new, different environment, it's time to start job searching (start here). If you truly are ready for a career change, there's still no need to panic. Just continue reading.

2. Major Discouragement

Deciding you want to change careers can be completely overwhelming. It feels like everything leading up to this point—your years of education, professional development, promotions, and late nights at the office—have all been a waste.

And so, you start doubting that you can do it. You start thinking that starting over is going to be ridiculously hard, that no one will want to hire you because of your lack of experience, and that you'll never be as successful as other people in your new field because you got such a late start. Maybe it's just not worth the risk.

Instead: Give Yourself a Pep Talk

Yes, changing careers is intimidating—but it's also very possible. (Want proof? Here are nine real-life stories.)

So, take a few minutes to pump yourself back up. Remind yourself that shifting your profession is normal and that very few individuals have a perfectly linear career path. It took a lot of hard work to get to this point in your career, and that's a great accomplishment. Now, you're going to move on to something different—an equally great (if not even better!) accomplishment.

A career change may be tough, but the reward—a job you love!—is worth it

Giving yourself a pep talk may sound cheesy, but it can be the push you need to convince yourself to go for it.

3. Resignation That You'll Have To Start From The Bottom

If you want to make a major career shift, your first reaction may involve a sigh of resignation as you assume that to actually get a job in your new target industry, you'll need to go back to school for at least another four years, apply to only entry-level positions, or submit yourself to an unpaid internship.

Instead: Identify Your Transferrable Skills

Making a switch doesn't mean you have to start from scratch. There was something that drew you to your initial profession, and if you hone in on that, you may be able to determine a new career path that closely aligns with your skills—but also provides that satisfaction you've been lacking.

For example, maybe you chose journalism as a major in college and your first career because you love telling stories. Now, you're desperate to get away from journalism, but it's likely that passion for storytelling is still alive—you just have to look for a different way to apply it.

So, maybe you become a marketing writer, and you tell the stories of a company's customers and how they benefited from the company's product or service. Or, maybe you freelance as a website copywriter and tell the stories of new businesses through their web presence.

By identifying the skills you can—and want—to transition to your new career, you'll be better equipped to explain to future employers how you'll bring value to their company without starting from the very bottom.

The general themes in all of these reactions are fear, uncertainty, and doubt. But deciding that you're ready to switch careers should instead incite a reaction of excitement—because this may be your opportunity to find a career you absolutely love

www.ingramcontent.com/pod-product-compliance
Lightning Source LLC
LaVergne TN
LVHW012112160826
845678LV00014B/3049
9798352466100